THE GNOSTIC TREE

By

Tau Synésius

THE GNOSTIC TREE

by
Tau Synésius
(Fabre des Essarts)

Gnostic Patriarch,
Primate of the Albigensians,
Bishop of Montségur
Grand Master of the Order of the
Dove of the Paraclete

Translated and Introduced by
Tau Phosphoros
Archbishop & Patriarch
Apostolic Church of the Pleroma

Fox Lake, IL

The Gnostic Tree
by Tau Synésius

Translated and Introduced
by Tau Phosphoros

Copyright ©2018, 2024 Tau Phosphoros
All rights reserved.

ISBN: 978-1-946814-07-4

Triad Press, LLC
123 S. US Highway 12 #33
Fox Lake, IL 60020

TABLE OF CONTENTS

Translator's Introduction	vii
Preface	ix
The Gnostic Tree	1
Complementary Pieces:	
The United Brethren	35
The Christ, by Grandmougin	36
Gnosticism and the University	40
End Notes	42

Translator's Introduction

The famous symbolist poet of the belle époque, Fabre des Essarts, was known within the French Gnostic milieu as Tau Synésius. Originally consecrated as Bishop of Bordeaux, he was elected to the Patriarchal throne of the Église Gnostique upon the sudden and unexpected abdication of its first Patriarch Jules Doinel, in ecclesia Tau Valentin II, in 1894. Although Doinel would return to the Gnostic fold in 1900 (as a bishop, but not as the Patriarch), *The Gnostic Tree* was written during the period of his absence.

The year of Synésius' patriarchal election, 1895, was also the year in which appeared for the first time a French translation of the *Pistis Sophia* (Amélineau). In the absence of the wealth of Gnostic writings that we have today, thanks largely to the Nag Hammadi discovery of 1945, the Pistis Sophia became a hugely influential work for the restored Gnostic Church. In 1898, just one year before the present publication, Papus (Dr. Gérard Encausse, in ecclesia Tau Vincent, Bishop of Toulouse) released a thoughtful and initiated exegesis of the Pistis Sophia entitled *L'Ame humaine avant la naissance et après la mort* (The Human Soul Before Birth and After Death) which we have translated and included in a collection of works by Papus entitled *Exegesis of the Soul: Three works on the nature, origin, and destiny of the human soul.* And in the very year of the publication in France of the present work (1899) appeared also a catechism by Tau Sophronius (Louis-Sophrone Fugairon, Bishop of Béziers) that was based upon the Pistis Sophia. These and other works related to the Church and to esotericism and occultism in general were being published rapidly during this period by Chamuel, another bishop of the Église Gnostique (Lucien Mauchel, in ecclesia Tau Bardesanes, Bishop of La Rochelle & Saintes). Given the fervent and intense activity of the bishops of the Église Gnostique of this period, it is difficult to imagine that the Church would splinter in a few short years, leaving the Église Gnostique ultimately unsustainable and creating a rift between the Patriarch and some of the greatest luminaries of the Church, including Papus and Tau Sophronius.

But in 1899, they are all working together to accomplish some of the most important work in the restoration of the gnosis. And this present work represents a much needed contribution at the time, to show the continuity of Gnostic thought from antiquity to the present. In spite of the dearth of knowledge concerning the original Gnostic sects and their writings - a lack which has been at least partially rectified thanks to the Nag Hammadi and other important discoveries - this work remains as relevant today as it was almost 120 years ago. We are delighted, therefore, that, like the tomb of C.R.C., this treasure may at last emerge from obscurity into the light of day, to inform and inspire a new generation of ecclesiastical Gnostics, the vast majority of whom are the direct descendants of the Gnostic Church of France; a church, like our own Apostolic Church of the Pleroma, which represented a truly *Gnostic Church*, not merely Christian mysticism clothed in the name of "Gnostic."

The Gnostics of today, whether neophyte or hierophant, will find a great deal of useful information packed into this brief essay. Synésius writes here as a true Patriarch of the Gnosis, leading us carefully through the mire of history to identify the golden thread of the gnosis in both the expected and some unexpected places; all while paying due respect to the past masters and martyrs of our venerable tradition. This work gives us insight not only into the general Gnostic doctrine, but also, and most interestingly, into the particular orientation of the Église Gnostique. It is my ardent wish and desire that all who read this short tract will be opened to the gifts of the Holy Spirit, most especially to the Holy Gnosis of our Lord Jesus Christ.

Tau Phosphoros
Archbishop & Patriarch
Apostolic Church of the Pleroma
June 30, 2018
129th Year of the Restoration of the Gnosis

The Gnostic Tree

T

I.N.S.P.

They have reproached Gnosticism for not having any unity of doctrine, and if the recent reconstitution of our Holy Church has not yet given birth to a new *Histoire des variations*, it is Bossuet alone who has been found wanting with respect to our enemies.

The reproach weighs heavy on our Pontifical Heart, so that we have long resisted the desire to respond thereto.

Within these few pages we have gathered concise accounts of all the Gnostic systems from their origin up to the present era, assured that this was the sole means of showing the indisputable unity of our Faith. In order to carry out this work, we have consulted the apologists and the adversaries with the same impartiality. Let us add that it is the latter who have furnished us the most ample material. We know, moreover, how limited the number is of Gnostic writings, the majority of the books of our masters having disappeared, not in the fires of Omar, which is but a legend, but in that of Theodose, which is a sad page of history. The truth will assert itself all the more victoriously to those who combat us, as our best arguments come from them and theirs.

If some lacunæ have been committed, some details neglected, some names forgotten, may we be forgiven, and let us be permitted to take for our own the well-known phrase: *Quæ falsa esse perspexeris respue et mihi qui homo sum ignosce.*

SYNÉSIUS
Pastor of the M.H. Gnosis

THE GNOSTIC TREE

When the germ of the Most Holy Gnosis fell from heaven upon the earth, there was at first a long and mysterious period of elaboration. It was, moreover, very difficult to establish even approximately at what period the event occurred. To refer to the recent discoveries of the scholars, which come always to confirm what the intuitives have presented, the **T** was a sacred sign since the neolithic epoch, evidenced by the various notched skulls found at the foot of the dolmens of Seine-et-Oise. These skulls bear at the sinopital region, very clearly marked, two small grooves forming the very august sign of our religion. We find this sign in the form of the *crux ansata* at nearly every latitude, and in the monuments of nearly every civilization, as well as in the hypogea of Egypt and the crypts of India.

But without wishing to remain any longer upon these fluctuating origins, nor penetrate into those dark depths where the work of germination is accomplished, let us hasten to enter upon the phase of external growth and glorious evolution.

It is proper, however, to study for a moment the concomitant or successive influences which have prepared the springing up and development of the immense Tree, which would one day cover the world with its branches.

A thousand philosophical and religious systems have come about from the sacred germ to thicken the fertile humus where it would fix its powerful roots or rather to pour out upon its nascent trunk the fertile waters that it awaited in order to grow.

It is the Brahmanic doctrine and its vast pantheism, it is Zoroaster and his ingenious theory of the two principles, it is Pythagoras and his Numbers, Plato and his primitive matter, source of all evil[1], Aristotle and his sole creative nature of the world, to the exclusion of the God of beauty and goodness, Hermes, and his bisexual Divinity. The Essenes themselves have played their part of precious collaboration, with their doctrine of the soul fallen from the heights of the subtle Ether into the darkness of Matter, as also the Neoplatonists and their divine hypostases. Philo, completing Plato and Pythagoras, brings about a powerful direction toward the concept of the Quaternary, of the Decad, of a God who creates only souls, leaving to the angels the organization of Matter. In their turn, the Therapeuts of Lake Maria supplied the sweet radiance of their social dream and their holy fraternity. As to Christianity, at first it mingled with Gnosticism, of which it is, on the whole, but the living envelope, and of which it reproduces all the contours - as is evident from the Gospel of Saint John - but the Johannite tradition soon degenerates upon contact with the Pauline pressure. The visionary of Damascus limits and endogmatizes the grand Christian idea. The Gnostic tree wishes to grow freely, outside of any narrow dogmatism, unto the serene splendor of the heavens. It breaks the husk and goes on to grasp the next root, a frail branch at first, that will be watered, sanctified, and fertilized by the blood of the martyrs, but which will not bend in the least under the politicism of Constantine, until it becomes ferocious absolutism, also an immense tree, sinister wood from which will be made all the gallows and all the pyres that the terrified world will see rise up, from Manes to Jan Hus and from Joan of Arc to Urbain Grandier.

Let us leave this antievangelical Christianity and return to the Holy Gnosis[2].

As it is principally from the side of the Orient that have come the various influences that we indicate above, it is in this same direction that the Gnostic Tree is going to deploy its most beautiful branches. It scarcely emerges from ground when a main branch shoots forth from its base, it is Nicolaism.

Nicolas, its apostle, was one of the seven deacons elected from the Church of Jerusalem. Born at Antioch, noble by birth, he is one of the first who had the courage to deny the direct participation of God in the creation. Saint Epiphaneus, that you are going to find each time that there is a calumny to concoct, a believer to insult, accuses him of horrible debauchery, that the coarseness of Latin may alone be permitted to describe. Clement of Alexandria, Theodoret, and Saint Augustine nullify most successfully the allegations of Epiphaneus. And this is all to their praise[3].

From that point, the great Tree of Knowledge is constituted: it has its mother- roots, its fibers, its living cells, its bursts of flowing sap, and we may henceforth study it in its most intimate substance. Without doubt there will appear more than once exfoliations, wild branches, we will see parasitical lichens, but in the depths of its organism, we shall find again always the same constitutive elements, and if, here and there, some erratic branches are going to draw into the ambient air some strange sap, it shall suffice to seize once more the true vital tradition to redescend the branch, to return to the trunk, and to reascend the consecutive branch.

The Gnostic Tree

Since its most remote origins, Gnosticism has posed four problems, and the dominating occupation of its apostles has been to resolve them:

1. Problem of the creation.
2. Problem of the divine incarnation.
3. Social question.
4. Question of women.

The seven following principles, which will be met with again in the final analysis, at the basis of all the Gnostic systems, as divergent as they may appear, have superabundantly resolved this quadruple problem. It is, according to the impeccable law of the Numbers, the Septenary which corresponds to the Quaternary:

1. Exclusion of the dogma of Creation, such as it is formulated by the Catholic Orthodoxy;
2. Existence of an inferior productive power of the Hylic World;
3. Doctrine of Emanation;
4. Grouping of the Aeons by Syzygies, that is to say by male and female;
5. Analogy of the three worlds- Pleroma, Ogdoad, and Hebdomad;
6. A Savior Christ, who is incarnated in Jesus, but who remains independent of him and leaves him before the drama of Calvary;
7. A redemption accomplished by the Holy Will of the Pleroma by which the woman will profit in the same measure as the man.

Such is the Gnostic unity. It is unnecessary to seek another. Unity in the great lines, in the orientation of the chief thought, of the evolutive thrust, infinite variety in the detail of the ecclesiastical ramifications.

And it is precisely this which gives to our Church this rich and magnificent glow, to which no religion immured in dogmolotry shall ever attain. We are the Knowledge, Γνωσις; now, Knowledge ought to be open not only to all established truths, but also to all the developments, we say even to all hypotheses.

After Nicolas, at the very time of the apostles, an immense branch crops up, which is going to mark an important phase in the evolution of the Gnosis, as much for the dogmas that it will fix as for the numerous ramifications which will emerge from it.

This is Simon Magus. Since the debut of our Church, he was able, by the sole force of his genius, to elevate himself to the concept of the Active Absolute, of which Fire is the symbol. He clearly distinguishes the two principles, Male and Female, forming pairs since eternity by Syzygies, and thusly poses the theory, so fecund, of the aeonic filiation. It is likewise to Simon that we owe the notion of the three worlds, and also that of the Demiurge, creator of man, considered by the Jews and the Christians as the supreme God.

As to the relationship of Simon to Helen, if it is not here a simple allegory, as claims Beausobre, it is then a symbolic reality, having the effect of offering to the disciples a striking image of the fall and recension of Sophia, and also to make them understand how the woman was a sacred thing, since, even fallen, she could become the companion of a great apostle. All the fables related on this subject by the Fathers ought to be rigorously discarded, as also the legend which makes of Simon a trafficker of holy things. If it is true that he offered money to Saint Peter, it could only be the legitimate remuneration for an ecclesiastical service, the obolus anticipated by a grateful brother and not the price of a celestial gift. But the Pauline orthodoxy was very glad to have a pretext to dishonor the one whose prestige so formidably overshadowed his own authority.

It is necessary to relegate to the same place the accounts which take the statue of the old Latin divinity *Semo Sanctus* for a monument raised to a divinized Simon. Pure legend, just as that ascension of Simon into the air and that miserable fall at the feet of the apostles!

In spite of all these slanders, and not withstanding all these pompous falsehoods, there remains no less to Simon the imperishable glory of having, since the beginning of the Christian era, posed the bases of the Gnostic doctrine.

Cerinthus, of Egypt, immediate disciple of Simon, while preaching an aeonology more confused than that of Simon, regards like him the creatures as the work of an inferior power, but he surpasses his master by clearly distinguishing the personality of Jesus from the Aeon Christos. The Christ had descended into Jesus only at the moment of his baptism and would have left him at the hour of his martyrdom; the Christ, being a spiritual being, could not logically suffer. This point of doctrine, first origin of Doceticism, we are henceforth going to see proclaimed by the majority of the Fathers of the Gnosis.

Menander, of Samaria, detaches himself like Cerinthus from the Simonian branch. He changes few things in the doctrines of his master,

The Gnostic Tree

however: to the symbol of Fire extolled by Simon, he adds that of Water and gives baptism in his own name. On the other hand, he introduces theurgy into the rites of worship. Simon had been but a mage, Menander was a magician. Magic, like doceticism, is going to become a new contribution which will be reproduced by many a Gnostic group.

Menander, in his turn, has brought forth two remarkable branches: Saturninus and Basilides.

Saturninus, Satorneilos, or Satornilus, according to the various hagiographies, of Antioch, is considered the father of Syrian Gnosticism. With him the dualism of Zoroaster appears in a very pronounced fashion. The kingdom of God and the kingdom of Evil co-penetrate one another at their borders. It is here that the world is born, work of the last seven Aeons or Demiurges. The Jehovah of the Jews is one of these Aeons. Man has emerged from their hands, like the rest of creation[4]. He is nothing in the beginning but creeping matter. A spark from the Pleroma falls upon him. He stands erect and thinks.

Sathan opposes to this sanctified creation a new man born entirely from him. From here come the two humanities, the Divine and the Sathanic, the Psychics and the Hylics.

The Demiurges revolt against God. From then on, the creature is separated from its superior principle. But Christ comes to save the Psychic man, by annihilating the action of Jehovah. However, struggle continues between the men of good (the Gnostics) and the men of evil (the Sathanics). Saturninus rejected the dogma of resurrection of the Body, as contradictory with the principle of the inferiority of Matter; a new truth that the subsequent Gnostics did not fail to publish in their turn.

Basilides, of Syria, proclaims before all the Pater Innatus, the one who is not born, Εν το Αγεννητον; this is the Supreme God, the sublime Abraxas, who extends into seven perfections and forms with them the most holy Ogdoad. These perfections or Aeons, by joining together, produce the Angels, grouped into 365 heavens. Now, this number is that given by the seven letters of the word Abraxas, taken in numerical value. The Angels of the last heaven, among which is Jehovah, have created the Earth, "the most impure of the worlds." Jehovah, that the common Jews have taken for the true God, is a jealous and cruel power who makes an iron yoke to weigh upon the world. Abraxas, the supreme God, sends the Prince of the Aeons, who incarnates in Jesus, whose mystical name is Calaucau[5], at the moment of baptism, with the mission of delivering men from the demiurgic tyranny.

In regards to the Savior, Basilides shares the docticism of Cerinthus, and like Saturninus he refutes the resurrection of the Flesh[6].

The work of Basilides was continued by his son Isidore, who had written a book of morals and another entitled the *Expositions*, from which Clement of Alexandria cites a long fragment.

As to the amulets called *Abraxas*, of which Chifflet has given a detailed nomenclature with figures to support it, they appear to us to be of Basilidean origin, whatever Beausobre may think of it. Basilides, without disavowing Menander, gives himself as a disciple of Glaucias - and not of Plaucia, as Proudhon writes – who himself would have received his teachings from the first Apostles of Jesus.

Saturninus had two disciples, Bardaisan and his son Harmonius.

Bardaisan, of Edessa, poet, distinguished erudite, knowing Syriac, Greek, and Chaldean, at first a fervent Catholic, soon evolves, denies the resurrection of the body, gives to Jesus a celestial body[7], "regarding the flesh, moreover, as eaten up with concupiscence," admits two origins of δυο ριζας the one good, which he calls the Good, the Light, the Right, the Merciful, the Pious, the Just; the other evil which he calls the Evil, the Darkness, the Left, the Cruel, the Impious, the Unjust; but for him God is the immediate author of the world. There is only the Demon that he has not created.

Harmonius, son of Bardaisan, preaches the paternal doctrine, while adding thereto that of metempsychosis.

But here we are far from our point of departure. By force of ramifications, the new branches have somewhat altered the primitive sap. Let us return by regressive path to the filiations covered, Bardaisan, Saturninus, Menander, Simon, and let us re-ascend the Gnostic trunk.

The study of these filiations that the logical progression has imposed upon us, has caused us furthermore to encroach upon the chronology, since the first branch which is now offered to us is Elxai, who flourished in the 1st century, whereas, with Bardaisan and Harmonius, we have arrived at the year 172.

With Elxai, or more precisely Elcesai or Eleasée, of Jewish origin, manifests a marked return to the Judaic traditions. Like the Hebrews, he observes the Sabbath, practices circumcision, and frequent ablutions. But contrary to them, he is horrified at the bloody sacrifices and rejects part of the Old Testament. Epiphaneus, according to his custom, addresses several grave reproaches to him; among others, he accuses him of having preached the denial by speech, on the condition that he had faith in his heart. As this same reproach will be later addressed to other Gnostics, notably the Templars, it may be supposed to be a question of a ritual ceremony, poorly defined, poorly understood by the profane. We shall have, moreover, the occasion to revisit this. Tillemont speaks of two Elcesaite sisters, *Martha* and *Marthane*, who would have been venerated as goddesses, and of a brother of Elxai, *Jexée*, who would have written several Gnostic books. It is Elxai, it seems to us, who introduced into Gnosticism the concept of the feminine sexuality of the Holy Spirit, conforming to the Hebrew word *Ruach*.

Carpocrates, of Cephalonia or Alexandria, bears upon his branch an efflorescence as strange as it is unexpected[8]. For him, our irreconcilable enemy is concupiscence. We must yield to it, under pain of being carried by it. We arrive at perfection only after having passed through all the works of the flesh. The community of women was necessarily indispensible, with a similar moral, which however did not prevent Carpocrates from being strongly attached to his wife Alexandria, with whom he had a son, that precocious genius to whom they have raised altars, that glorious Epiphaneus, dead at age seventeen, after having written a remarkable work on justice, and which merited him the honor of being regarded as one of the fathers of communism.

With Carpocrates, as with his predecessors, we find the dogma of the Deus Ingenitus clearly formulated, as also that of a world created by inferior powers. They claim that the Carpocratians burned their ear lobes in order to recognize one another. They have the honor of having made in the temple a place for esthetics, by exposing therein the images of Jesus, Pythagoras, Plato, and Homer. Saint Epiphaneus, so as not to yield to his customs, attacked Carpocrates and his homonym Epiphaneus with an unprecedented violence. Around 160 a Carpocratian, Marceline, brought to Rome the ideas of his master.

If from Carpocrates we pass to Marcion of Sinope, as the chronological order would have it, the contrast at first inspection appears striking. To the sensualism of Carpocrates, he opposed a rigorous asceticism, which goes so far as to proscribe the use of wine in the Sacrifice. He extolled fasting, martyrdom, and virginity. He rejected, furthermore, the majority of the Judaic ideas, attributed the visible world to a sovereign power, author of evil, and admitted metempsychosis and magical works. Saint Epiphaneus, with his usual amenity, treats him as a pernicious serpent. He had no less numerous disciples for it, and Marcionism existed for many long years[9]. The aeonology of Marcion is very close to that of Valentinus, at whom we are soon going to arrive.

With his disciple Apelle, the opposition between the two testaments is asserted even more energetically. Faithful to his mission, Gnosticism moved further and further from Judaism[10]. For Apelle, the God of the Jews is a perverse God. The world, which does not reflect the infinite goodness of the true God, could not have been his work. It is in order to mitigate the horrors of this sadness here below that Christ has come. Apelle recognizes, however, that the visible world is a clumsy copy of the angelic world, and thus poses one of the fundamental principles of the Gnosis: THAT WHICH IS BELOW IS LIKE THAT WHICH IS ABOVE.

As to that Philumene, Φιλουμενη, whose inspirations Marcion, madly in love, followed, she could only have been, as Renan has most judiciously observed, but a symbol of philosophical truth.

Metrodorus, another disciple of Marcion, suffered martyrdom under Emperor Decius.

Cerdon, of Syria, taught two principles. From the Good principle emanates the spirits, which tend toward happiness; from the Evil principle are born the bodies, origin of all sorrow. The Mosaic law, with its superstitions and bizarre practices, is the work of Evil. The Christian Law, with its Saints and sublime prescriptions, is the work of the Good. Cerdon added that the suffering of Christ had only been apparent. He vigorously continued the tradition of the anti-Judaizers.

Cainism is a frail branch, which detaches itself from the Gnostic trunk around 150[11], without bearing great fruit, nor founding a very long-lived family. It pursued even further the anti-Judaic tendencies of Cerdon. For the faithful of the doctrine, all the cursed personages, Cain, Ham, Esau, etc., are pneumatics. If the Old Testament maltreats them, it is for the sole reason that they have revolted against the Judaic Jehovah. This is precisely their glory, declare the Cainites; we must honor them. Quintilla, according to Tertullian, preached this singular gnosis in Africa, an unavoidable fit of truth in delirium, provoked by the desperate efforts of the Judaizers on behalf of their ferocious God.

Valentinus, of Pharbe (Egypt), of Jewish origin, is the greatest luminary of the Gnosis. Proudhon considered him, with just reason, as the most profound of the philosophers. Whether or not he received his teaching from Theudas, disciple of Saint Paul, he has nevertheless fixed,

The Gnostic Tree

in a definitive fashion, the immutable part of the doctrine. The parallelism of the three worlds, Pleroma, Ogdoad, and Hebdomad is very clearly established by him, It is he who is first elevated to the true concept of the Uncreated Eternal, Bythos, the Abyss, the Proarche, the Propator, living outside of space and time, yet real, and incontestably more distinguishable by reason than the Ουχ ων, God of certain Alexandrians.

The Aeonology, still flowing with its predecessors, is asserted in a serene clarity. We see here the Triad generated by the Unity, Father, producing itself the holy Ogdoad, the Decad appearing in its turn, and completed by the Dodecad, the Union of the Aeons by Syzygies, the Mystery of the Loves of Sophia, that of her grievous fall, of her redemption by the Aeon Christos, the birth of Achamoth, fruit of the mad passion of Sophia for Bythos, the birthing of the Demiurge, blundering organizer of the World, the distinction of the Pneumatics, the Psychics, and the Hylics, the future annihilation of the unconscious and lamentable creations of the Demiurge, the impossibility of the resurrection of the flesh; all these truths are found luminously presented in the system of Valentinus.

He likewise created a liturgy which contained four sacraments:

The Mystery of the redemption of sins;

The Baptism of smoke;

The Baptism of the Spirit of the Holy Light;

The Great Mystery of the Seven Tones.

It is he who fixes the six degrees of Gnostic Initiaiton[12]:

> Borborians;
> Coddians;
> Soldiers;
> Phibionites;
> Zacheans;
> Barbelites,

to which it sufficed to add the diaconate and the episcopate, with the Albigensians, to complete the Ogdoad of perfection.

It is likewise he who has revealed to us the various mystical signs and seals of the different degrees.

The eucharist under both species, and the use of balsam oil for the unctions also played a part in his system of worship.

It seems that the Gnostic Tree has been exhausted in giving that immense and glorious branch, on which we have just given a moment of our thought. However, it is not. Other branches are going to shoot forth, which will bear new sap and will produce new fruits. These are first the Ophites and their chief Euphrates, whose profound theosophy will be filled with universalist tendencies. Without positively returning to Judaism, they borrow some concepts from it and make every effort to determine a harmonic fusion between the notions of the Old Law, the Magianism of the Chaldeans, and the mysticism of Plato. For them, moreover, as well as for Valentinus and his predecessors, all flows from one unique, infinite principle, understood through the reason[13]. Tillemont sees in them the "doctors of Manichaeism." They seem indeed to have made it their business to instill in the doctrine a certain extension in the demiurgic sense, and they give a true aeonology of the Hebdomad. Their Demiurge is Ialdabaoth, generated by the Darkness, himself father of Iao or Jehovah, who in his turn begat Sabaoth, who begat Adonai, who begat Eloi, who begat Ouraios, who begat Astaphaios.

It is Ialdabaoth who created man, but he becomes jealous of his creature while seeing it rise into the light, and from this jealousy is born Sathan Ophiomorphos, like, in the Pleroma, Achamoth was born from the desire of Sophia.

This Ophiomorphos becomes the tempter and the evil genius of man. He must be vanquished by opposing him with the brazen serpent, the genius of the knowledge of Good and Evil, otherwise called the Holy Gnosis. From here comes the name of the group, and also the use of the serpent in their ceremonies, but by virtue of pure symbol, of course.

The little branch of the Antitactes, who come next, have only a very secondary importance. Anti-Judaizers, after the manner of the Cainites, they would have pushed the hatred of Jehovah even further than those latter; the Fathers of the Church accuse them, indeed, of having overtly practiced adultery, for the reason that the God of Moses condemns it. But the accusation is suspect.

Prodicus, of Egypt, and the Adamites, his disciples, constitute a most original branch, that Beausobre, by a strange anachronism, confuses with the Manichaeans. We need not take this any further, as he does the same for the Cathars of Germany, the Patarins of Italy, and the Turlupins of the Netherlands.

Their name of Adamites comes from a ritual concept, which may seem bizarre, if we place ourselves at the point of view of the current morality, but which certainly had its aesthetic side. They placed themselves, in order to pray, in a state of complete nudity, claiming that no ornament equals the beauty of the human body in the eyes of the

Eternal, and furthermore that Adam and Eve were nude in Paradise. This custom did not prevent them, moreover, from living very often in a state of absolute abstinence, as Clement of Alexandria himself declares. Saint Epiphaneus, who is not suspect of indulgence, adds that they drove out from their sect those who fell into lasciviousness.

Among their books of predilection is cited the Interrogations of Mary, a work which could very well be none other than the Pistis Sophia of Valentinus. They also had, so it would seem, a Gospel of Eve, and another Gospel called of Perfection. They were accused of having practiced the community of wives. But this is the reproach that the Fathers invariably address to all the sects which have not admitted the indissolubility of marriage.

Montanus, of Ardaban (Phrygia), outside of the idea of the next coming of the Paraclete, which he did not cease to maintain with his disciples, does not seem to have caused the Gnostic Tree to flower with any new dogma. What he renewed - and he did it with passion - was worship and morals. Numerous fasts, absolute abstinence from the work of flesh, and xerophagy were imposed upon the believers. Communion was no longer performed but under the species of bread and salt.

Renan determines that with their mysteries was mingled an orgiastic and corybantic element[14]. What is certain is that there are those who established the ceremony of the Weepers, which, in some regards, recalls our Consolamentum. Seven virgins vested in white and carrying torches entered the Church while uttering lamentations. All the faithful wept with them, and fatidic cries were exhaled from their breast.

The Montanists practiced baptism by immersion, the neophyte being completely nude. They gave themselves willingly to theurgical works, they possessed the gift of incantation and prophecy, and madly sought martyrdom. The town of Pepuze, in Phrygia, today destroyed, was their holy city. The faithful went there from all points of the world, and delayed not to constitute there a numerous group, which soon radiated unto the entirety of Asia and even unto a part of Gaul.

Montanus was always accompanied, in the course of his apostolic missions, by two young women, Priscilla and Maximilla, who had for him a tender affection and who supported him with their prophetic and consoling words.

As pure as had been the religion of Montanus, it was nevertheless exposed to the slanders of the Fathers. Cyril accuses the Saints of Pepuze of celebrating their Passover by cutting up a child into small morsels, which they devour, after having previously dredged them in flour. Saint Isidore declares Montanus personally convinced of adultery: but he was a eunuch! These believers, who so willingly sealed their faith with their blood, abhorred shedding that of others. They went so far, in this sentiment, as to refuse military service. This example will not be lost, and thirteen centuries later will bear its fruits with George Fox and the Quakers, a true reincarnation of Montanus and the Saints of Pepuze[15].

We know that Montanism made an illustrious recruit in the person of Tertullian, who for this ground escaped canonization. According to Tillemont, Pope Victor himself would have been one of its adepts for a moment. The small church existed, moreover, up to the end of the 6th century, and produced various branches which are called the Phrygasts, the Cataphryges, the Pepuzians, the Tascodrugites, the Quintillians, and the Artotyrites.

The branch of the Encratics, with Tatian, of Assyria, as protagonist, approaches the previous, not only by the date, but also and especially by the spirit of continence and renouncement. From here comes their name of Encratics, that is to say Continents. They proscribed the use of meat and wine. Even in the sacrifice they employed only water, which explains the name of Hydroparatasts that they were sometimes given.

More taken with doctrines than the Montanists, they formulate anew a doctrine long since immutable in Gnosticism, to understand the subordination of the creative power to the absolute power, of the Demiurge to Bythos. They also proclaim the pure appearance of the body of Christos.

From Mesopotamia, where it originated, the Encratic branch was diffused into Cilicia, into Asia Minor, at Rome, and into Gaul. Among the disciples of Tatian, they cite Julius Cassien, who, they say, dreamt of the suppression of the sexes, and Severus, apostle of the Severians, who considered Saint Paul as a dangerous heterodox, an opinion underpinned by the modern Essenes[16].

Hermogene admits the eternity of inorganic matter. God organizes it, but it constantly infringes upon the laws that he imposes on it. This is a new concept of the Demiurge, but at the foundation it is always the same dogma of a power foreign to God, clumsy or criminal, generating Evil. Hermogene had two disciples who continued it, Hermias and Seleucus.

Around 180, the Gnostic Tree shot forth a vast branch from the Occidental side. It seems that Providence had condensed in it all the sap remaining nearly idle from this side, up to the era that we are in. It is a question of Marc and the Marcosians, that because of a nominal analogy, they have often confused with Marcion and the Marcionites.

Marc posed the existence of the two Principles, asserting the Divine Quaternary composed of the Ineffable, the Silence, the Father, and the Truth, and declared, like the majority of the Fathers of the Gnosis, that Jesus had died only in appearance, and that the resurrection of the flesh was an illogical doctrine.

Such is the essence of his doctrine. We rediscover here all the principles so often formulated, and it is a proof, moreover, of the unity of our Faith. Marc, like so many other Gnostics, practiced Magic. This is one of the crimes that the Church of Rome hardly ever forgives[17]. From this comes all of the violence thrown up against him by Saint Irenaeus and Saint Jerome. A demon necessarily had to have assisted him in his marvels!

Marc exercised a considerable fascination upon the women. But nothing authorizes the belief that he abused it. He made use of it in order to attract them into his church, knowing how the woman is a precious agent in matters of apostleship. They have indeed spoken of a sort of mysterious initiation which consisted in introducing the profane into a nuptial chamber, where the Initiator proceeded with spiritual marriages reproducing cells of the Aeonic Syzygies. Renan even goes so far as to conjecture the following dialog between Marc and the neophyte: "From me you are going to receive grace. Prepare yourself as a bride who receives her bridegroom so that you may be what I am and that I may be what you are. Prepare your bed to receive the seed of light. Behold the grace which descends unto you. Open your mouth. Prophesy.

- But I have never prophesied. I do not know how to prophecy!

- Open your mouth, I say, and speak. All that you say will be prophecy."

Were it authentic, this dialog would only imply, on the whole, a very acceptable theurgy, analogous to that which is still practiced today in various eastern sects, having nothing, moreover, in common with Gnosticism. We recall that at the moment of the sacrifice[18], Marc took a chalice full of pure water and following fervent invocation, the water was changed into blood.

The Marcosians made in their ceremonies unctions of balsam oil and composed therein what they called *Apolytroses* or *Redemptions*.

These are the first among the Gnostics who were given, we believe, the title of *Parfaits* (Perfects), declaring, "that they drank the plenitude of the Gnosis of ineffable virtue."

The Marcosians stretched from the Rhone to the Garonne, had a religious center at Autun, as there appears the Greek inscription of Ιχθυς, a study of which we have given in the *Initiation*, and even passed beyond the Pyrenees, if we are to believe Tillemont.

To this branch of Marcosism, perhaps should be attached the physician Alexandre and Alcibiade the Phrygian, who long edified the Lyonnais by their pious practices and in whom the work of creation inspired a profound horror[19].

Concerning the Archontics, they appear to us, in spite of Tillemont, to derive only very indirectly from the Marcosians, if it is true that they considered the woman as the work of Sathan. Moreover, they barely went beyond Crete and Armenia, where they had originated. The only point which interests us is that they admitted a sort of resurrection of the Soul.

We must return to the Orient, where were developed at nearly the same time as Marcosism, two successive branches, which deserve an honorable place in this nomenclature.

First are the Theodotians, named thus because of the synonymy of their two Apostles, Theodotus the Currier, and Theodotus the Banker. The Fathers accused them of having rejected the divinity of the Word, but it is more probable that, like their predecessors, they considered Jesus as the momentary receptacle of the divine influx. Their originality consists above all in having introduced into the Gnostic hagiography the great name of Melchizedek.

Praxeas, who comes next, spoke out against the trinity of the Roman doctrine, and was forced to place the Gnosis upon a purely philosophical terrain, by giving to the Aeons an ideal existence. But, at the base, his heterodoxy is only apparent. Between the Aeons of Valentinus and the living ideals of Plato, which were like those of Praxeas, there is but a difference of word.

After the Theodotuses and Praxeas, the Gnostic Tree remained unproductive for a long period. It does not seem, indeed, that during this interval the least shoot had sprouted from its bark. They say that it collected and concentrated itself, purified and fortified its sap, with a view of some near and imposing parturition.

We see, indeed, toward the end of the 3rd century, an immense branch shoot forth in one stroke from the eastern part of the old Tree; a branch which would bear some of the most radiant flowers and the most savory fruits that the Holy Gnosis had given up to then.

We have named Manes and Manichaeism.

An Arab named Scythian, possessor of a considerable fortune, had come to install himself at Alexandria in order to study occultism there. He wrote four books there that he bequeathed to his disciple Terebinthus. This latter withdrew into Persia, where he became the husband of a rich widow, to whom he left the books of Scythian on his death bed.

If we are not certain of the birthplace of the great ancestor of the Albigensians, we are even less sure of his name. Was he called Corbicius or Cubricus, as some claim? Urbicus as asserts Saint Augustine? Carcubius, as Beausobre advances? For it is scarcely at the moment of his apostleship that he appears to have taken the name of Manes, the Thinker, the Living Thought (from min, men, *mens* in Latin) or of Manichae, the Consoler, the Paraclete (from *Manahem*, in Hebrew). Born into slavery, he was redeemed by the rich widow, who had inherited the books of Scythian and who saw to gift them to her young friend.

Manes appears to have established himself towards this era at Seleucia or Ctesiphon. His existence is, unfortunately, known to us only insufficiently. The Fathers speak to us of his theological discussions with Marcel, ex-consul, and especially Archelaus, orthodox bishop of Cascar; and from their accounts arise in the faith the courteous moderation of the Christian laity and the unbridled brutality of the men of the Church[20]. It is quite possible, though the fact is not historically established, that Manes had accompanied King Sapor as physician, in the course of his military expeditions. It is from this that he would have drawn and maintained that holy horror for war, which constituted one of the essential points of his doctrine.

In these sentiments, he could not have failed to incur disgrace from the prince, all the more so that his humanitarian flights were aggravated by evangelical predictions. Pursued by the wrath of Sapor, Manes had to take refuge at the palace of Arabion.

But he later found some esteem under Hormisdas, successor of Sapor. In 273, Bahram succeeded Hormisdas, and Manes was persecuted anew for having confessed the name of Christ. It was certainly under this king that he gained the glory of martyrdom.

Historians are not in agreement on the nature of his torture.

According to Saint Epiphaneus, he would have been flayed alive with the tips of reeds and his skin would have then been filled with straw. Others determine that he had been crucified, and that his body, cut in two, had been placed at the two gates of the city.

It remains to us to speak of the doctrine, the morals, and the manner of worship preached by Manes and his disciples.

Manes enlarged again the aeonology of Valentinus, already so vast and deep "God," he said, "was in the supreme heaven, accompanied by his Blessed Aeons, whose *number cannot be counted*, nor duration marked."

The Aeons fill all: outside of the Pleroma there is only the Shadow, the Void, the Kenoma[21]. For Manes, God has made from all eternity the invisible world in which he resides. The other, the visible world, is the work of time. It is imperfect, corruptible, and must one day disappear. All the souls will be saved, because all are made from the celestial substance.

The Serpent of Genesis is none other than Christ, the Divine Spirit, the God of total knowledge. It is absurd to believe that the Eternal had forbidden man to taste of the fruit of the Tree of Knowledge. The majority of our evils come from concupiscence, which itself derives from Matter, where the human soul is entombed, but from which it is to emerge triumphant.

Manes and his disciples, notably Hierax and Papus, were the moralists of the Gnosis. They have that glory of having achieved the work of the Carpocratians, the Ophites, and the Marcosians, by teaching that outside of the relative, transitory, conventional moral, there is an absolute, eternal, and fixed moral. It is this moral which caused them to condemn war, as hostile to the precept of the Decalogue: *Do not kill!* And contrary to the doctrine of the one who commanded to Peter to return his sword to its sheath. Strange statement! This hatred of war is one of the things for which Saint Augustine most vehemently reproached them. It does not seem, moreover, that the words of Jesus had ever had a very vibrant echo within the bosom of the Catholic Church. I see on the contrary the majority of its pontiffs celebrating the praises of the frightful Sabaoth and grovelling at the feet of conquerors, from Clovis to Charlemagne, and from Charlemagne to Napoleon, when they are not themselves directly practicing human butchery, like Richelieu, Sourdis, and Lavalette![22]

Saint Augustine likewise accuses the Manichaeans of holding conception in horror, and of systematically using their wives in a manner so as not to have children. The accusation is perhaps a little doubtful, even though it had been renewed by Pope Leo I; but it is quite certain that for the disciples of Manes, sexual union, when it was fruitful, was considered as a collaboration with the work of the Evil Principle.

Documents on the cult celebrated by the Manichaeans are missing for us, but it is plausible to imagine it analogous to that celebrated later by the Albigensians, their direct descendants. They had temples adorned with the symbolic Serpent, under the form of the Ouroboros, or perhaps coiled around the looped Cross. They practiced a eucharist which has remained mysterious up to now, and that the Fathers of the Church, according to their traditional amenity, treated as an abominable debauchery, whether these pious Romanicoles had taken literally some ritual text, or that they had invented every piece of their slander[23]. As to the sacerdotal costume of Manes, we know that it was composed of shoes half white and half green, probable image of the two principles, and a multi-colored cloak (the εματιον ανθινον, of which Straban speaks).

The Manichaean initiation comprised three seals[24], one on the mouth to signify the purity of their speech, another on the hands to attest to their innocence, the third upon the breast as a symbol of the holiness of their morals. The Manichaeans established twelve disciples and a patriarch. These disciples elected seventy-two bishops, who, themselves were charged with electing the priests and deacons.

Manichaeism already had numerous adepts in the lifetime of Manes, but when his doctrine received the consecration of his martyrdom, it spread unto the furthest borders. India itself had its Manichaean apostle, in the person of that Thomas, whom they have often confused with the incredulous disciple of the Gospel.

Priscillian, who brought the good news into Spain toward the end of the 4th century, was truly only a detached branch of Manichaeism. He was of high birth and possessed a remarkable talent for oration. Fought against in turn by Idace, bishop of Merida, and by Hygin, bishop of Cordoue, because Priscillian had the gift of later gaining Gnosis, then condemned as a heretic by the Council of Saragossa, he is finally ordained bishop of Labile by Instantius and Salvian. The numerous conversions that he carried out excites the furor of his enemies[25]. Idace and Itace made appeals against him to the secular power, and despite the intercession of Saint Martin, he is dragged to Bordeaux with some of his disciples and condemned to death. The Gnostic martyrology is increased by a new saint, and as in the time of Manes, the blood of the Martyr causes a new season of flowering to bloom. It is probably from this epoch that the preaching of the Gnosis in Germany and Bohemia dates. We know indeed that these countries still counted many Priscillianites in the 6th century, since a council held at Prague judged it necessary to renew against them the fulminations of the Council of Saragossa. If we take the word of the text of the various judgments which have condemned them, the ritual practice of the Gnosticism of the Priscillianites was reminiscent of the Adamites; like them, they prayed naked. As to their doctrine, it appears to have reproduced that of Manes. We know that Priscillian exercised, like Marc, a sort of fascination over women, by his genius and his beauty, which contributed powerfully to multiplying proselytes around him.

We are now going to enter into a long period of unfruitfulness. The exuberant virtuality which produced so many and such beautiful branches loaded with such luxuriant flowerings, stops abruptly, as if a mysterious force had suddenly paralyzed the old Gnostic Tree[26], and dried up within it the source of life. For there is scarcely room to cite the few meager twigs, the few diffuse groups who are going to succeed one another from the 5th through 10th centuries, more parasites of the Gnosis than flesh of its flesh; more lichens and sporadic fungositics than living branches[27].

Such are the Circoncellions, who push the furor of martyrdom to the point of replacing it with suicide[28] when it does not come to them; the Audiens, who worship an anthropomorphic God; the Macedonians, who deny that the Holy Spirit is co-eternal with the Father; the Apollinarians, who contest the existence of the human soul in Christ; the Luciferians, who preach a rigorous asceticism; the Messalians, who condemn manual labor; the Jovinians, who proclaim the equality of all merits; the Vigilancians, who proscribe the cult of the Martyrs; the Jacobites, who give birth to the Coptic Church; the Corrupticoles, the Phantasiasts, the Agnoites, and a thousand others[29].

We need not speak, of course, either of the Novatians, who present us only with a diminished Montanism, or of Arius, since his narrow Gnosticism - he recognized but two emanations - detaches completely from our holy traditions; nor of Nestorius, who considered Christ as a deified man; nor especially of Eutyches who claimed that the Divinity had suffered in Jesus.

We would like to stop here for a moment at the noble and valliant Synésius, that tender friend of Hypatia, that proud patriot, that his fellow citizens forced to accept the episcopal see of Ptolemaeus, and who knew how to preserve, in the exercise of his official functions, all the purity of his personal beliefs and all the touching ardor of his familial affections. Our ritual has preserved a part of his hymns, and his name occupies an honorable rank within the Gnostic hagiography.

We repeat, the Gnosis is going to enter into a long period of painful sterility. But the Holy Tree perished not because of this. It rose silently through the darkness that the Byzantine decadence and papal absolutism made thick around it, similar to those stalks which shoot forth from the back of caves, straight and firm, without buds or branches, until they have found the light of the heavens through the opening of the air-hole.

Behold the coming of the great blossoming, the superb and glorious branch, reddened with the blood of so many martyrs and which would bear so many green hopes and so many white flowerings! It is from the direction of France that it has aired itself and thus come to console us, from all those interminable periods of darkness and silence. The Orient has given the Gnosis all that it may give: it is henceforth the turn of the Occident. It is up to the Occident to nourish the sap of the old Tree, to shed upon it the treasures of its gentle skies, and to make rise along the fibers of the sacred oak the vivifying ardors of its virgin soil!

Let us not exaggerate, however, the glory of our beloved land. The Gnosis, as we have seen, had already visited Marc and his disciples, Priscillian, and many others perhaps whose names have been lost, but whose work did not remain unfruitful. It would be to fail in our duty as veracious historian to assert that Albigensianism - for it is on that which we wish to speak, it is understood - issued forth entirely from the entrails of France. It is probable that there were, at various points of Europe, modest groups, little chapels, which piously kept the seed of Truth, and that it is from them that emerged that magnificent movement of the 12th and 13th centuries, of which our provinces of the South were the theater.

We must not forget that the Bogomils preached their Cathar doctrine at Constantinople in the 11th century, and that the bishop Basil, their chief, received there the crown of martyrdom under the Emperor Alexis Commene; or that around the same era, a Gnostic episcopate was founded in Dalmatia, while the Gnosis penetrated into Italy, with the apostle Gundulf and the bishop Girard. There was even, at Milan, an auto-da-fé of Cathars.

Ardent missionaries soon spread into Aquitaine, Poitou, Champagne, Flanders, and Orléans. Orléans had had, since the 11th century, its Gnostic branch. A holy woman come from Italy, probably a disciple of Gundulf, had brought our doctrines there. It happened what always happens when a woman becomes an apostle; the proselytes abounded. Several members of high Catholic clergy converted, notably Lisois, monk of Saint-Croix, Etienne, theology professor of Saint-Pierre, old confessor of Queen Constance, Theodore and Herbert, their friends.

The Cathars of Orléans proceeded directly from Manes. Dualists and Docetists, like him, they brought to bear a great courage in the affirmation of their beliefs, recommending themselves by an extreme purity of morals[30], and a probity most rare, in that frightful year one thousand that signaled so many horrors and terrors.

Richard, Duc de Normandy, instituted a violent indictment against them, in the service of King Robert, his suzerain. The compliant and too-feeble spouse of Constance was himself charged with interrogating them[31] and wanted, through terror, to try to lead them back into the Catholic bosom. But he clashed with unshakable convictions. Lisois and his companions invited with all their voices the martyrdom with which they were threatened.

They were satisfied. It is while singing hymns that they marched to the rack. The hecatomb was composed of thirty victims. This is the first which was offered in France to the sacerdotal minotaur. How many will follow, alas!

They relate that the frightful Constance recognized her confessor, who marched at the head of the retinue, set upon him like a fury, and pierced one of his eyes with the tip of a switch. This horrible ferocity was repeated nine centuries later at Paris by a noble lady from the Monceaux quarter, in the course of anti-communist reprisals!

Public malignity had caused to fall upon these glorious martyrs the same accusations as upon the Nicolatians and the Marcosians. It is claimed that they practiced the most abominable debaucheries, slaughtered babies, and fed on their flesh. Lamentable gossip of history! It is always the same savage hatreds against those who know how to die for their ideals, always the same return to primitive atrocious animality!

The masterwork, or rather the vibrant epic in prose, that Napoleon Peyrat dedicated to the Albigensians, is, like every poem, a work where fantasy holds too prominent a place. The author has not grasped the direct link which attaches its heroes to orthodox Gnosticism. Possessed by the desire to create an epic book, which takes place entirely within the period which extends from the death of Pierre de Castelnau to the Council of Latran, he has not seen that the history of the Albigensians was but one act - the most beautiful, it is true - of the great touching drama, which begins with Simon Magus and which will end only at the end of the ages, or rather, in order to preserve our image unto the end, the most majestic branch of the Tree, which has its roots in the depths of divine Reason, and whose top touches the heavens.

Peyrat claims that the Albigensians proceeded neither from Bardaisan, nor Basilides, nor Valentinus. He has barely recognized in them a vague kinship with the one that he calls "the poetic Marcion." He no less recognized therein that their Christianity is a "knowledge" and not a sacrifice, and that their chief was the teaching Word and not the suffering Man-God, that they reject the Hebrew Jehovah, the Mosaic Bible, and that finally, like the Manichaeans, they worshipped the Mani, that is to say the Holy Spirit.

But are these different points not the very substance of the doctrine of the Gnostic apostles, to which Peyrat claims that the Albigensians are strangers? It suffices, as a response, to peruse our exposé. Yes, the Cathars of Albi, the martyrs of Montségur and Béziers, Guillabert de Castres, Vigoros de Bacon, and Esclarmonde de Foix, are indeed the direct descendants of Simon and Valentinus!

It is true, moreover, according to what the author asserts elsewhere, that Albigensian Christianity is neither in the Jewish tradition of Saint Peter, nor in the Greco-Roman tradition of Saint Paul, and that, if these venerated Gnostics extol an apostle, it is uniquely the mystical Saint John, "the most Platonic and the most eastern of all the disciples of Jesus." But does not this very assertion singularly confirm what we say? If Basilides, Bardaisan, and Valentinus were Christians, it is, I imagine, neither in the manner of Saint Paul, nor after the fashion of Saint Peter. Had they another gospel than that of Saint John?

The region which extends between the Mediterranean, the Pyrenees, the valley of Tarn, and the upper course of the Garonne, was designated among all to become the theater of a religious renovation. In this country had been mingled the Iberian, Gallican, Roman, Saracen, and Gothic blood[32]; that is to say that it had become a hearth of powerful intellectuality. Since 1167 a council of Manichaean bishops had been held at Toulouse, under the Presidency of Nicetas of Constantinople. Numerous assistants had come there from the borders of Bulgaria, Hungary, and perhaps Bohemia, where the eastern Gnosis had never ceased to have altars, since Tatian and the Encratics.

One of the most immediate fathers of Albigensian Gnosticism, that holy personage, Eon de l'Estoille - predestined name! - who after having long lived as a hermit in the forest of Brocéliande, heard there one day a mysterious voice, that of Merlin the Enchanter, who told him to go to mass[33] and to listen to the first words of the Gospel. Now, these were the words: Per Eum qui venturus est! Eon believed himself designated by the word Eum, which resembled the Latinization of his name. He abandons forever his cell and his forest, takes up his staff and traverses France, while preaching the Holy Gnosis. He delayed not to gather numerous disciples.

Our intention is not to recount here the history of the Albigensians. This writing, once again, is but a simple exposé of doctrines, an attempt at dogmatic synthesis, nothing more. For the events of the grand drama, we shall limit ourselves to referring our readers to the book of Peyrat, which, with regard to the purely historical, is a work of profound truth and high conscience.

A gathering of the Friends of God took place around 1208, at Montségur, under the presidency of the patriarch Guillabert de Castres. It is there that they would decree the essential points of the doctrine and the details of the liturgy. The Albigensian hierarchy admitted two degrees in the priesthood: the diaconate and the episcopate. The bishop had as acolytes two grand vicars, the Major Son, and the Minor Son. A place of honor was given to the women, who would occasionally become priestesses of the Paraclete, and who in any case very often fulfilled the functions of deaconesses. This admission of women to religious charges is further evidence of the relationship of the Albigensians with the Gnostic groups of the first three centuries. The Cathars of Albi do nothing but continue Simon, Marc, and Priscillian.

The little town of Montségur became from then on the Gnostic Rome. Its steep and rugged Plateau was Mount Capitolin des Manilus of the holy Cathar army, "the see of the Priesthood, the asylum of faydits, the refuge of the alms-houses, of the schools."[34]

The Albigensian doctrine, we repeat, conforms absolutely, as concerns its main lines, to that of the primitive apostles. An unknown, inconceivable God manifests itself through its Christ, which has burst forth like the dawn from the depths of its Essence[35]. His mother is not Mary, but Mani, the Divine Thought. The body of Christ was purely sidereal. It is Lucibel, a sort of fallen angel, the Demiurge of the Valentinians, who has formed the world. It is fitting to note that the Albigensians, as did Synésius besides in his hymns, give the name of

Demiurge (Demiourgos) to God considered as Son, emanator of souls; a simple verbal convention, which changes nothing in the theological concepts. Christ must one day restore the rehabilitated Lucibel to heaven. The Paraclete is the promised consoler, "the regenerator of the world, the creator of perfection."[36]

The morals of the Albigensians were very pure. They must be classified among the continent groups. I am well aware that they have been reproached for having renewed and put into practice the famous adage: *Ab umbilico ad pedes homo non peccat*; but we have the right to ask their accusers whether they have not cited a truncated text. It would suffice indeed for there to follow two simple words: *contra Deum*, in order to make of the phrase the expression of an indisputable truth. It is most certainly from the head and heart exclusively that come the sins against God, and not from the senses.

As to the form of worship, it presents all the imposing simplicity of the primitive Gnostics. The office took place on Sunday. There they read the Gospel of Saint John, accompanied by the commentaries of the Officiant, then they said the Pater. Then came the ceremony of consecration, the Supper, and the kiss of peace. The liturgy contained a certain number of genuflections and silent adorations. There was, moreover, neither musical instrument, nor vocal hymns. Each year they celebrated four solemn feasts:

1. *Nadal*, or Noel, which recalled the appearance of Christ in the world;
2. *Pascor*, which commemorated the return of Christ into the bosom of the Pleroma;
3. *Pentecosta*, which had as its aim to recall the advent of the Paraclete;
4. *Manisola*, which was a sort of feast of the dead, during which they prayed for the misguided and the afflicted, by calling upon them the Consoling Spirit.

They had four annual fasts of forty days each. Outsiders were admitted to the Albigensian agapes, without previous initiation; they received the consecrated bread and wine, and they performed with them the supreme rite of the kiss of peace. This generous hospitality did not come without introducing more than one ferocious wolf into the flock, and thus hastened the hour of the grand martyrdom.

We shall say nothing of these horrors. If our readers call into question the account of N. Peyrat to whom we refer them once again, they may be fully edified in reading the book by Pierre de Vaux-Cernay, who could not be suspected of having any sympathy for the Albigensians, I imagine. Each of its pages sweats blood.

It remains to us to say a word on the ritual detail which has caused the Albigensians to be seen as sectarians of paganism in the eyes of their inept contemporaries. The Albigensians proscribed the Cross as a religious symbol. This custom conformed absolutely to the holy Gnostic doctrine: the cross, indeed, can only invoke the remembrance of Jesus dying, that is to say of Jesus separated from the Aeon Christos. It was important not to let the Parfaits and Parfaites stray from the faith, by divinizing an instrument of torture that the divine astral body had not touched. It is in the name of the same logic and by the same measure of prudence that the Vaudois likewise rejected the symbol of the cross, a proscription that the protestants would later reproduce, but without comprehending the philosophical and religious bearing.

The Templars may only seriously be attached to Gnosticism beginning from 1291, date of the fall of Saint-Jean-d'Acre and their departure from the Holy Land.

Although the basis of their doctrine emanates, from the beginning, from the Johannite tradition, we cannot in good conscience claim them as our own, so long as the massacre of the Infidels was one of their preoccupations, not to speak of their daily occupations.

It is, unfortunately, very difficult today to penetrate unto -their true doctrine, through the multitude of accusations leveled against them by their enemies, the ones bloody or ignoble, the others simple grotesque. O. de Cruise, who has dedicated a curious memoire to them, throws into relief the state of soul of the papacy at the period of their trial. "The court of Rome," he says, "protected the philosophy of Averroes, which was a sort of atheism. This same Pope, Clement V, who let the Templars burn, refused to see burned the Commentary of this Arab on Aristotle." We see by this what strange partisan spirit animated the Roman Court, against the Knights of the Temple.

As to that famous Baphomet, Baffomet, Baffometus, from the Greek Βαφη μητους, which they venerated and which has had them seen as idolaters, this could well be but a reproduction of the ophiomorph emblem of the Ophites and the Manichaeans. An erudite German claims that the Baphomet is a crouching sphinx with the appearance of a woman. In this case, there would be room to attach the Temple to the Egyptian orientation; to the Valentinian group perhaps.

The Gnostic Tree

The historians of the Templars cite certain details of the Initiation which would be more than improper with regard to current ideas, notably the ceremony of the four kisses that the candidate had to give to the Officiant, *in tine spinæ, in umbilico, in virga virili, in anu nudo sine medio*. If this strange practice has ever been followed, it could have had no other aim than to inspire in the neophyte the scorn of his flesh and to symbolize his absolute submission to the rules of the Order.

The crucifix upon which the neophyte had to trample and spit was again, without a doubt, a symbolic ceremony; perhaps a simple means to permeate his spirit with one of the fundamental dogmas of Gnosticism, namely that the Christ was no longer in Jesus at the moment of the passion, or to show him that God made allowances for denial by word of mouth, according to the doctrine of Carpocrates and Elxai, and that the great sin was to abandon it from the heart. "The sins of the spirit affect God much more than the corporeal ones," says later the Jansenist Saint Cyran.

The details of the trial of 1311 regrettably allow to remain all of the obscurities surrounding the history of the Temple. Five hundred knights, in the midst of torture, acknowledge as true the accusations leveled against them[37], though some of them recanted afterward. But where is the truth? In the avowal or in the retraction? The accused, with the aim of shortening the torture, could have acknowledged the exotericism of their practices, the obscene kisses, the insulted crucifix, etc. Then, rather than expounding upon the esoteric doctrine, or even regretting having revealed their symbols, they claimed to have lied. such may well be the history of Jacques Malay and of the Commander of Normandy.

The Council of Vienna, which condemned the doctrine of the Templars, fulminated likewise against the *spirituals*, who considered Saint Francis as a reincarnation of Christ, against the *Beguines*, who appeared to be the faint continuers of Carpocrates, and finally against the *Fraticelli* or *Frérots*, who renewed the Gnostic communism of Epiphaneus.

We arrive at one of the most persistent, perhaps one of the most ancient, and undoubtedly one of the most interesting Gnostic branches : Valdéism.

This group may go back as far as the 3rd century of our era[38]. Formed by the Christians of the Johannite tradition who escaped the persecution of Emperor Decius, a first node would have been constituted in the valley of the Alps, which separate France from Italy. From here probably comes their name of *Vaudois*, otherwise called the *inhabitants of the valleys*. The name of the great apostle of the 12th century, Pierre de Valdo, would have been, in this case but a simple surname, Pierre the Vaudois. This name, moreover, presents the most varied forms among the authors: Valdo, Valdio, Baldo, Baldon, Faldensis, and even Falidisius[39].

Charvoz, archbishop of Lyon, who has written a work on the Vaudois, claims that the group goes back no further than 1100. But his book is pure quibble, which cannot invalidate the common opinion.

The Vaudois are sometimes designated under the name of *Pauvres de Lyon* (the Poor of Lyon - trans.) and of *Insabottati*. The first arises from the fact that they were a numerous group in this city and because Pierre de Valdo was originally from there. The second is explained by the pious ecstasies which were customary to these believers, prolonged intoxication of the soul, stirring the remembrance of the orgiastic cult of Bacchus *Sabazius*, and no doubt also the magical *sabbat*, two words which are, moreover, very closely related. The common word *sabot* would have the same origin, the Vaudois being generally, by a spirit of humility, shod with *wooden shoes*[40]. There still exists at Autun an order of Nuns, the Ladies of the Retreat, that the popular language calls the *Sabotte* sisters. Could this not be a confused reminiscence of the ancient Vaudois, unconsciously stored in the minds of the people who allow nothing to be lost! Whatever be the origin of Valdéism, what must be said to its praise is that it was able to preserve through the centuries all the purity of its doctrine and its original rites. The Vaudois, of whom M. d'Oppède made, in 1545, so complete a massacre, thanks to the collaboration of his honest galley-slaves and to the aid of the no less honest cardinal de Tournon, professed identically the same faith as the believers gathered in the Italian valleys, in the time of Decius.

Their morals are of the most elevated. Like the Manichaeans, they are horrified at the effusion of blood. War is for them such an atrocious thing, that they considered as murderers not only those who fought the Infidels, but even the popes and bishops who preached the crusades. To pronounce a sentence of death or to see it executed is a crime against God[41]. Inexorable logicians, they adopt the letter and the spirit of the Gospel, and refuse to take up arms, even in the case of legitimate defense. They proscribed oath-taking absolutely, an example that the Quakers would later follow. We have seen Parfaits (for the Vaudois gave themselves this name too) face torture and death, rather than swear: the oath was considered by them as a sort of profanation of the divine name and as a violence committed against his will. They condemned individual property. For them, humanity forms but one sole and unique family. The grouping of peoples into distinct states, into enemy nationalities, is an absurdity. In short, it is the communism of the Gospel asserting itself in its simple sublimity. It is the Christian utopia marching audaciously towards its realization.

Among the Vaudois, as among the Albigensians, the Marcosians, the Priscillianites, etc., etc., women could exercise the fullness of the ministry. They were opposed to baptism being given to infants, claiming that a human being cannot be incorporated into any church without their free will consent. Marriage is an absolutely free union; either spouse may leave whenever they wish.

As to the forms of worship, it was reduced to some very simple ceremonies: preaching, a confession, which seems very analogous to our Appareillamentum, and the eucharistic consecration. This consecration took place either by virtue of the evangelical words, or, according to Eberard de Béthune, by those of the *Pater* repeated seven times. The Vaudois denied all power to the unworthy priests. They scorned the excommunications of the Catholic Church, declaring that God, the Supreme Shepherd, may alone exclude a sheep from the flock.

What is capital in the tradition of the Vaudois, and what gives the greatest honor to this holy and glorious Church, is that it was the first to proclaim that truth that THERE MAY BE PRIESTS ORDAINED BY GOD, AND THAT ANY LAITY WHO OBSERVES THE FAITH IN ITS INTEGRITY MAY RECEIVE THE SACERDOTAL CONSECRATION DIRECTLY FROM HEAVEN.

At the example of the Albigensians, the Vaudois did not allow singing in their ritual practices.

Such were the morals, the doctrine, and the form of worship of the disciples of Pierre de Valdo, until the middle of the 16th century. Around this period the protestant influence caused the religious orientation of those who still survived from the frightful massacres of 1545 to deviate somewhat. We believe, however, that there still exists in this period, in the lands of the Cévennes, some modest groups where the true Valdésian tradition has been piously preserved.

Jan Hus ought also be claimed as one of our own. In the midst of the universal religious disorientation produced by the disorders of the grand papal scheme, he was able to point out the true path to the Believers. He was before all an apostle of charity, striving to unite the souls into a common act of faith and adoration. To lead the Church back to the primitive simplicity of the Gnostic schools of Syria and Egypt was his heart's desire and the aim of all his thoughts. It had to be realized. Bohemia, his homeland, embraced his doctrines with ardor. He wanted the Parfaits to seek the rule of their conduct and their faith in the evangelical precepts, and for the validity of the sacraments to depend upon the morality of the priest who administers them[42]. The odious trafficking of indulgences wrung cries of indignation from him, and, a new Jesus, he stigmatized the new merchants of the Temple by the breath of his anger[43].

Frightened by the success of his preachings, and more particularly preoccupied by this latest reformative tendency, an old privateer, become pope under the name of John XIII, decreed the major excommunication against Jan Hus. The iniquitous procedure of the Council of Constance delayed not in echoing the pontifical fulminations. Summoned to appear before this assembly erected in high inquisitorial court, he left Prague by favor of a safe-conduct pass that Emperor Sigismond had delivered to him. But, in spite of all the human laws, he was arrested upon his arrival at Constance and thrown into a horrible dungeon, from where he was drawn only in order to hear the Fathers of the Council bellow against him the most ferocious list of charges and to condemn him to burning. His friend and disciple, Jerome of Prague, braved the fury of the assembly, in order to share the torture of his master.

The crime was consummated on July 6, 1416. We know the sublime end of the heroes, so divinely related by the beautiful verses of our great Victor Hugo. But Victor Hugo, some say, was an abominable heretic, very suspect of partiality in favor of an enemy of the Roman Church. So be it. Allow me to cite, then, *in extenso*, another author: "Hus and Jerome boldly endured death; they marched to their execution as to a feast where they had been invited, and none of their words betrayed the least defiance. When they began to burn they intoned a hymn that the flames and the violence of the people alone interrupted. No philosopher has welcomed death with the same courage as they who braved the pyre!" These are the words of Eneas Sylvius Piccolomini, who was pope under the name of Sylvester II!

There would still be some great names to cite besides Jan Hus and Jerome of Prague, notably those of Procope the Great, Jean Zyska, and Jean Rokysansky. But it would be to deviate us from our plan to relate the war of the Hussites, as they themselves deviated from the true

The Gnostic Tree

tradition, which condemns propaganda by force of arms. Once more, it is a simple study of doctrines that we wish to present to our readers[44].

After the death of Jan Hus, the Holy Tree resumes its calm and silent growth, through the succession of the centuries. Protestantism, under its double Lutheran and Calvinist form, although grafted unto the Hussite branch, could not be considered as a Gnostic branch. Similar to the branches of the baobab, instead of standing erect towards the heavens to go and draw therefrom the true light, it descends towards the earth, taking root there and soon living its own and independent life. The upper part was detached definitively from the Gnostic Tree, and an abyss exists today between it and us[45]. If it has, in a certain regard, freed the human thought by breaking with the Roman yoke, it has resolved on a lamentable return to the past, by prostrating itself blindly before the bloody works of the biblical Jehovah, by taking its delight in the reading of the Old Testament, and by renewing the Judaic tradition, from which Catholicism itself had been semi-liberated. On the whole, and all things considered, Protestantism was, in the religious order, a regression rather than a progression.

Moreover, if, doctrinally, we are not drawn towards Protestantism, it seems even less disposed to come to us. Is it not one of the luminaries of the Reformed Church, M. de Pressensé, who, republishing and resuming all the wrath of the orthodox Fathers against our glorious Communion, has written this unforgettable phrase: "Gnosticism is the nightmare of Humanity!"

But, they are going to tell us, if you reject any relationship with Protestantism, where do you want us to go seek the Gnostic tradition? What is that marvelous Tree which grows silently in the shadows, if not a fiction of poetry, an inconsistent and ungraspable chimera? If it no longer produces flowers, nor fruits, nor branches, it is because it is dead and well dead!

To this we may respond, by supporting ourselves upon Plato, that the Ideal, even outside of the actions which realize it, has a proper existence which resists every blow and emerges radiant from every lethargy. The Gnosis is an ideal; the Gnosis cannot die.

But outside of this absolute existence, is it not possible to find here and there, in the order of contingencies, proofs of the existence of Gnosticism over the course of these last three or four centuries? Quakerism, to which we have made more than one allusion, Mormonism itself with its doctrine of feminine emancipation, the Quietism of Mme.

Guyon, that mystical Helen of that other Simon Magus, who is called Fénelon, this Quietism which so easily absolved the sins of the flesh, the Jansenism of Saint Cyran, who made so large the part of women in the ecclesiastical reformation of which Port Royal was the theater, and who led his father back to the holy communism practiced by the Marcionites and the Vaudois, Babeuf, with his egalitarian republic, Enfantin and his Priest-Couple, Fourier and his desperate efforts with a view to establish the harmony of the Pleroma in the midst of the hylic hebdomad; aren't these so many Gnostic remembrances, adventitious sprouts appearing on the surface of the Old Tree of Valentinus?

But none of these churches has possessed the integral Gnosis. At the most they have inherited some fragments of its doctrine, some vague tendencies of its faith. In this last quarter of a century, which has seen such ruin carried out, it has borne witness to the rebirth, or rather to a new epiphany of the Gnostic truth.

A man of high intelligence had felt, since 1867, mysteriously devoted to the propagation of the new good. He remained meditative for many years, plunged into study and prayer, not yet finding himself sufficiently armed for the noble struggle that he was going to undertake.

But his hour finally came, and Valentin II appeared to the men of good will, filling France with the works of his second apostolate.

The skeptics - and God knows our era abounds in them - did not fail to ask him who his consecrator was. Who has made you pontiff? From whom do you hold your powers? Who has transmitted to you the pallium and the Knosti?

Valentin could have, at the example of Fabré Palaprat[46], the restorer of a pretended Templar religion, imagined a sacerdotal filiation seeing his powers of initiation go back to Simon or Cerinthus.

But he preferred to tell the truth: "It is the Aeon Jesus himself who laid hands on me and consecrated me bishop of Montségur[47]." This declaration absolutely conforms moreover, to the tradition of the Vaudois: THE PRIESTHOOD MAY BE CONFERRED IN ALL ITS PLENITUDE BY A SIMPLE DIVINE INFLUX WITHOUT THE ACTION OF ANY INITIATIC SIGN.

Thanks to the noble ardor of the new Patriarch, the Gnostic Church was promptly reconstituted. A special era, dating from the common year 1890, was first of all proclaimed. This year corresponded to the 1st year of the Restoration of the Gnosis. Then they proceed to the organization of the forms of worship, the restoration of the three sacraments, the

Consolamentum, the Breaking of the Bread, and the Appareillamentum, and the Gnostic hierarchy was re-established by the nomination of eleven titular bishops, one of which is a sophia, that is to say a female bishop, and a great number of deacons and deaconesses.

Montségur was chosen as primatial see, in remembrance of the Holy Mountain upon which two hundred martyrs were burned in 1224 by the Satanic will of the Inquisition.

In the month of September 1893, the bishops gathered in synod confer the See of Montségur to Valentin II. Some days later, the Martinist Order was associated to the very high Synodal Assembly.

Here is the nomenclature of the episcopal dioceses which have been in full exercise since 1893:

Montségur,
Toulouse,
Béziers,
Concorezzo,
Paris,
Milan,
Rennes,
Warsaw,
Lyon,
Bordeaux,
Carcassonne.

The Order of the Dove of the Paraclete was then created in memory of the Faydits and the Knights and Dames of the Albigensian war, and the Very Holy Martyrs of the Inquisition of the south.

The year 1894 - Year V of the Restoration of the Gnosis - was marked by a harrowing defection. The Patriarch Valentin, without anything having forecast his determination, abjured the Gnostic faith to enter the hands of the Roman bishop of Orleans. But a patriarch is always similar to the golden branch of Virgil; our holy tree has not delayed in seeing to appear a new one. Synésius, previously elected and consecrated bishop of Bordeaux, has been promoted to the Primatial See by a decision of the Holy Synod, and it is he who since the abjuration of Valentin II directs, with the grace of the Holy Aeons, the destiny of the Gnostic Church.

Four new episcopal sees have been created. They are those of Bulgaria, Perpignan, Orleans, and Bohemia, which today brings to fifteen the number of the members of the Holy Synod.

Such is the history of the Gnostic evolution, from its furthest origins up to our day. So, if we now recall the four problems stated at the beginning of this work, namely:

The problem of creation;

The problem of the incarnation;

The social question;

The question of women,

it will suffice to recollect the exposition of the doctrines of our holy apostles so that the four solutions requested appear with a luminous clarity.

To the problem of Creation, Gnosticism responds:

The physical world is the work of an inferior power; it is too badly made, too full of contradictions and horrors to have emanated directly from an infinitely good and just being.

To the problem of the incarnation, Gnosticism responds:

The Aeon Christos descended from the Divine Pleroma has been incarnated in Jesus in order to save the Psychics of good will, but once his preaching was accomplished, he returned into the bosom of the Pleroma, and not at all suffered the tortures of Golgotha.

To the social question Gnosticism responds:

There is but one human family, whose every aspiration ought to extend to cursing war and marching incessantly towards a harmonic communism.

To the question of Women, Gnosticism responds:

Woman is the equal of man, the undisputable *parhedre* of the anthropomorphic Syzygy, and as such she has the right to exercise the fullness of the priesthood and, in this way, the vessel of infirmity, of which the Catholic Church speaks, becomes the vessel of election of the Gnosis!

The duty of the Parfaits and the Parfaites, of the Deacons and Deaconesses, of the Bishops and Sophias, who will carry on with us, is luminously traced in the depths of their conscience: it is to spread around them the Gospel of peace and truth, to multiply themselves in fraternal works, so that each day more numerous, the souls, those divine birds, come to rest their wings upon the branches of the Holy Tree!

COMPLEMENTARY PIECES

THE UNITED BRETHREN
(Moravian Brethren)

Beside Jan Hus and his friends, it is not irrelevant to cite the sympathetic United Brethren, whose origin seems to go back to the 4th century, period of the preaching of Methodius and Cyril. These noble believers constituted, in 1457, a very long-lived society, harmoniously organized, where the most pure communism of the initial Gnosticism was practiced. They had then for a primate the old curé Michel Bradacz. Driven out of Bohemia by King Ferdinand II, they took refuge in Moravia, from which they are again expelled in 1627. They then establish themselves on the borders of Saxony, thanks to the high protection of the Count von Zinzendorf. Later, various Moravian groups emigrate into America, where they still exist as patriarchal societies, which are at once commended by their ardor in the works of clearing land, their cordial union, and the purity of their morals.

One of their great apostles was Jean Amos Komensky, better known under the Latinized name of Comenius. Born in Moravia, around 1592, of very modest extraction (his father was a simple miller), he undertook great theological and literary studies.

Attracted early on by the beauty of the Moravian doctrines, he followed the brethren in their various emigrations. Charged with the direction of the gymnasium of Leszno, he published there the *Labyrinthe du Monde*, book of apostolic elan, true gospel of the people, where the potentates of every rank are mercilessly flogged.

We find him again later at Upsala, where he lives in the intimacy of the grand minister Oxenstiern. He then returns to Poland, where he presides for some time over the destiny of the Moravian Church. The Swedish-Polish War of 1655 obliged him to exile himself. He came to die, full of days, at Amsterdam, in 1671, leaving after him the remembrance of a saint and of a friend devoted to humanity.

Tau Synésius

THE CHRIST
by Charles Grandmougin
(Gnostic drama)[48]

Is Ch. Grandmougin initiated into the mysteries of the most holy Gnosis? There is a secret there that we hesitate to penetrate. Moreover, in the case in point, as everywhere and always, all is in all; whether the poet had wished it or not, his work is no less one of the most beautiful Gnostic dramas which have been meditated and conceived, and the soiree of February 28, where it was given to us to hear it for the first time, left in the soul of the spiritual Shepherd of the Parfaits and Parfaites a sweet and indelible memory.

The curtain rises on the fresh landscape of Nazareth; Jesus, in whom flows deliciously the essence of the Christos, wishes to see again the cradle of his human childhood. He is with his mother. Tender words are exchanged. The remembrance of old and innocent joys haunt his soul, and the whole past seems to come alive again for him "in those old pathways where he still finds the familiar detours, in those long white walls, in those lilacs and rosebushes with sweet perfumes."

> I am happy: my head with sweetness leans
> On your shoulder, and I, prophet triumphant,
> I am become again your infant!

Exquisite things, all filial, all softened by the momentary awakening of man; but behold that all of a sudden the radiant Aeon appeared and the Christos stands up in all his divine height:

> It is that a higher duty has made of me its prey
> And that to the divine order my soul has responded.

His majesty will burst forth just now, more intense, more imposing still, when he will cry out before his detractors - his former friends - felled by a gesture of his hand:

> Froth without respite, somber souls that excavate
> Envy, spirits limited by your resentment!
> Your laughter of demons betrays your torments;
> I am not come to dazzle the town...

And further on:

> Adieu, natal land, and paternal house,
> Land where human ingratitude is eternal,
> Where the impotent drool, where the jealous writhe,

The Gnostic Tree

> Adieu, you that fear is going to keep on your knees,
> Adieu, you who might love me...

In the second scene, we are with Magdalene, I was going to say with Sophia. She is, indeed, this amiable sinner, with that poor Zenon that she abandons, quite the suggestive symbol of the final Syzygy of the most august Pleroma. Like Sophia, she soars up toward the Supreme God, toward the Abyss of Forbearance and Puissance that she has glimpsed in a dream of love.

> ...Your gentle eyes sow pure rays;
> Your luminous and sublime serenity
> Overcomes me each day, burns me, and I am engulfed
> In the adoration of your sacred charms.
> The calm nights, the oppressive middays, the gilded evenings,
> All for me to relate to you, and your absence
> Fills me, and my gaze submitted to the power
> Of a persistent glamour, that nothing may banish,
> Populates the desert places of your remembrance.

But Jesus understands all that is hylic, sensual, in the passion of Magdalene; he gently rebuffs her:

> I do not know,
> Woman, whether I read well into the depths of your thoughts.
> But I sense in your eyes, the splendor of which adores me,
> An unconquered flame where evil still lives.

Little by little, under the influx of divine radiance, the love of the sinner is purified and idealized. Like the other Sophia, finally conscious of her error, she curses her carnal ecstasy of the first hour, renounces her mad delirium, and falls, grown through repentance and vivified through redemption.

Third scene: the Garden of Olives. Here is going to be asserted, in all its truth, the doctrine of our great apostles, Cerinthus, Valentinus, Saturninus, Elxai, the Ophites; Christos, in his quality of divine being, could not suffer.

The hour of anguish is come. He reascends unto the splendor of the Pleroma, leaving Jesus to his sufferings. The man alone remains, but how great still! It is the church abandoned: the altar is deserted, the organs are mute, but what majesty under its high ogives, and what infinite sadness its old melancholic stained-glass windows weep. One senses that God has passed through here!

Of Grandmougin's poem, this part is, according to us, the most beautiful, because it is the most human, the most intensely lived. The desperation of Jesus is depicted with extraordinarily powerful images. We would like to be able to cite the entire piece:

> Oh! speak to me, pure night, Oh! answer, Stars,
> Frightful infinity, rend me your veils,
> For my ears listen and my eyes want to see;
> I call in desolation the sweet certitude
> Whose clarity must read into that solitude
> And reveal in me the fevers of duty!
>
> Oh! Doubting oneself and having no more a guide!
> Crying madly under the blue of the empty sky
> Open to my gaze as a yawning chasm!
> Thinking that our life is a horrible dream,
> Which, without having any aim unfolds and is completed
> Between two infinities where hovers the nothingness!

O earth, devour me, if the heavens have deceived me!

Also quite beautiful is the scene of the arrest. Here, as in many places, the poet has rigorously followed the synoptics. But for the very basis of the doctrine, as the good Gnostic that he is - or that he would deserve to be – he has referred to the Gospel of John, which is, as we know, our book *par excellence*.

In the scene entitled *Pilate*, the Syzygy Jesus-Christos is resumed anew. The dialog between Christ and Pilate is of an incomparable beauty. The intervention of Magdalene at the moment of the judgment, which is not mentioned in any gospel, not even the apocryphal ones, is very likely a conception, and which, moreover, has great merit in our eyes, to recall to us Sophia definitively pardoned, transfigured, and re-entering into grace with Bythos.

Grandmougin has us likewise bear witness to the remorse of Judas, condemned irrevocably by Mary and by Magdalene, but absolved by Jesus, which is, moreover, in perfect accord with the Cainite and Marcionite doctrine. It was contrary to the generous soul of the gentle poet to damn irremediably the man who sold the One whose religion was love!

The scene of Golgotha is incontestably the most dramatic. The dialog between the mother and her Divine Son wrings tears, however engulfed one may be in the hylic mire. Here again, according to the

Gnostic orthodoxy, the Aeon Christos has left Jesus, and his Humanity exhales a desperate and sublime lamentation:

> Ah! why have you abandoned me, my God?
> My mind and my body agonize together;
> My final offering is human; I tremble
> Like a child lost in the night of the paths;
> Horrible visions pass by; the morrows
> Are sketched out beyond the ages, innumerable;
> I hear the confused cries of the miserable people,
> That they torture in my name, under heavens left dull,
> And who rage with horror, while seeking my succors!

The scene of the apotheosis or resurrection comes entirely from the Gnostic ideas, unless it is not to be interpreted in the symbolic sense, and that the author has not had the sole intention of thus representing the eternally living Christian ideal in the world. This lyrical dialog is, besides, beyond comparison, with regard to form, and melodiously concludes this beautiful drama.

Such is the work of Ch. Grandmougin. Posterity will certainly give him a place of honor in the glorious Anthology that it will extract from the frightful heap of literary productions of this century. The future will speak of the *Christ* of Grandmougin, as we speak of the *Prométhée* of Eschyle. For the Gnostics, it will become a classic book, that the Parfaits will read with veneration, and which will serve as mystical bond between the Poemander and the Pistis Sophia. In return for his noble work, may our Brother Grandmougin receive our patriarchal benediction and upon him and his may the grace of the Aeon Jesus, Celestial Flower of the Pleroma, descend!

SYNÉSIUS
Gnostic Patriarch

Tau Synésius

GNOSTICISM AND THE UNIVERSITY

From one of the most beautiful books which have been written by a university pen (*Histoire de la Philosophie* by Alaux), we extract the following lines, which shall serve as epilogue to this book:

"Gnosis is knowledge; the Gnostics are the men who understand, who know, and who have the explanation or the secret of things.

"The Infinite Being, source of all beings, is the invisible incomprehensible Father, that indeterminate Principle of all that exists, that obscure foundation from which all emerges, the abyss, Βυθος. From the abyss, from the Infinite Being, emerge the beings, less and less perfect, from the most elevated unto the most humble, descending step by step, all following a continued degradation. They constitute two worlds, the one celestial and divine, empire of the good, where reign Light and Life, the other inferior, empire of evil, darkness, and death. The first beings emanate from the Infinite Being, manifestations distinct from what is confused in the abyss; distinct forms, various names of the Unique Being. These are the Aeons, Αιωνες, eternal intelligences, the ensemble of which is, with Him, the intelligible world, the divine world, the Pleroma. The Aeons are classified into series, conforming to the ancient theories on the numbers, and go by syzygies, or by couples, two by two. The least perfect, the least divine of the Aeons, is the one who produces, or who organizes the inferior world: this is the Demiurge, still divine, already terrestrial, last emanation of the Pleroma, first power of the inferior world, bond of the two worlds.

"This world where we live has therefore not been created by the Infinite Being, by the Unknown Father, the Abyss; it is the work of the Demiurge, imperfect, miserable work, mixture of light and darkness, of good and evil; a work unworthy of the Father and destined to perish. In this inferior and perishable world, are imprisoned the souls, in expiation of a primitive crime. The fall calls for a Redeemer, not the Demiurge whose unfortunate work must be reformed, but one of the high powers of the Pleroma. The Divine Thought, the Divine Word is made man in order to enlighten man and teach him the way of return to God. This is Jesus Christ, antagonist of the Demiurge, reformer of his plan, destroyer of his creation. Jesus has not come to accomplish, but to abolish the old law. The author of this law is Jehovah, the Demiurge. The old law expresses the thought of the Demiurge, the Christian law expresses that of the Unknown Father, of

God. The other men worship the Demiurge, the Christians worship God. Among men, the ones captivated by the inferior world are Hylics (υλη) or material: such are the pagans; the others, who aspire to the divine are Pneumatics (πνευμα) or spiritual: such are the Christians; those who are elevated only unto the Demiurge are the Psychics (ψυχη): such are the Jews. The Hylics will perish; the Psychics will obtain only the limited and temporary blessings of the Demiurge; the Pneumatics alone will enter again into the bosom of the eternal Pleroma, into the Kingdom of Heaven."

FIN

ENDNOTES

1. According to Plato, God is the orderer, the harmonizer, and not the φυτουργος.
2. Cf. the very interesting work of Papus: *Traité méthodique de science occulte*. - G. Carré, publisher.
3. It is apropos to remark here that the Gnosis contains two distinct morals that, throughout the ages, perpetuate two parallel currents, the *Continents* and the *Epicurians*. Mr. Léon Maury, in his thesis on Gnosticism, has therein very clearly traced the tendencies and the character: "If the material is the source of evil, it is necessary to deliver ourselves therefrom and to reduce as much as possible the connections that we have with it. From here comes asceticism, and this asceticism has been practiced with the most extreme rigor by several sects. Or else, and here is the other term of the alternative, since nature is by itself evil, one ought not trouble oneself with the sensible world. One ought to dream only of the superior things and for the rest follow the natural impulses."

Let us say it once and for all, it is elsewhere than upon the terrain of flesh that one must seek the unity of the Gnostic moral. It is in the hatred of war, in fraternity, altruism, universal compassion, the evangelical community: sentiments common to all the Gnostic groups without exception.

This dualism, which is going to assert itself more and more in the course of this exposé, is at least as acceptable as the present contradictory moral, which on the one hand charges with infamy the woman who gives herself to anyone, and on the other hand has almost admiring indulgences for the runner of gallant adventures. Lucrecia Borgia is as good as Don Juan, or else the moral is but pure convention!

4. E. Renan. *Orig. Christ.*
5. This word signifies: Hope upon hope.
6. The Sarcosome of Jesus Christ, says a contemporary Father of the Gnosis, is not resurrected. That of no man shall resurrect to rise into the heavens. There is no place in heaven, that is to say in the pure ether, for the carnal flesh! (Dr. Fugairon, my 2nd, to Fabre des Essarts, on the person of J.C., *Initiation*, July,

1897.)
7. Eusebius.
8. Amélineau.
9. E. Renan, *Orig. Christ.*
10. E. Renan and Vacherot.
11. Proudhon, *ces. et Christ.*
12. Amélineau. - Several Catholic writers have clumsily taken the names of these various degrees for so many Gnostic sects.
13. Proudhon.
14. E. Renan, *Orig. Christ.*
15. Justified in the faith by the essence of evangelical thought and by the criterium of Kant, this doctrine is philosophically indisputable. Recently renewed by the Doukhobortsi of Russia, it has had the implicit approbation of that great humanitarian, who is called Czar Nicolas.
16. Cf. the *Messies Esséniens*, by Garredi.
17. E. Renan.
18. De la Magne.
19. E. Renan.
20. Beausobre.
21. Beausobre.
22. It seems, however, that within the very midst of the orthodox Roman Church, there was a truly evangelical tradition. This manifestation is unfortunately too rare. Let us take the opportunity to recall the noble words of Waso, bishop of Liège, to his confrere de Chalons, who urged him to exterminate the heretics: "Imitate the Savior; tolerate those who stray from the true faith. That which is naught but dust ought not judge the dust. Let us not seek to take the life of the sinners by the secular sword; for we, who are called bishops, *have not received in our ordination the sword of the children of the age*." This holy pastor lived in the time of King Robert. (Cit. by Henri Martin. *Hist. de Fr.*)
23. Beausobre.
24. P. Blanc, *Théol.*
25. Pluquet, *Dict. des Her.*
26. We must make an exception for the magnificent branch of the Albigensians, who perhaps originated from the 3rd century and which grew in the shadows for long years, but which had its

complete expansion only in the 13th century. We shall speak on this later.

The same observation, with some reserve, is to be applied to Valdéism.

27. Cf. Matter, *Hist. du Gnost.*
28. César Cantu, *Hist. Univ.*
29. P. Blanc.
30. H. Martin, *Histoire de France.*
31. Raoul Glaber, *Chr.*
32. Michelet, *Hist. de France.*
33. Michelet, *Hist. de France.*
34. N. Peyrat, Op. cit.
35. Ibid.
36. Peyrat.
37. Vast, *Hist. de l'Europe.*
38. Muston.
39. Peyrat.
40. Littré declares the origin of the word sabot to be unknown, yet, on the other hand, the examples of the use of this word that he cites are all subsequent to the appearance of Valdéism.
41. These Huguenots had professed since the 12th century the reputedly modern doctrine of the unity of the human race, just as they preceded our era in denying the legitimacy of the death penalty, so freely and barbarously dispensed in their time. (Sudré, *Hist. du Communisme.*)
42. H. vast.
43. We recommend the reading of the Review *Le Spiritisme moderne*, where, with an eloquent breath of the soul and noble puissance of style, our friend and brother Médéric Beaudelot expresses ideas on God and Humanity very near to our own.
44. See the note *in fine*.
45. It is sometimes necessary to make a reservation on the subject of liberal protestantism, which by curtailing the narrowness of Calvinist protestantism, has come sensibly nearer to us.
46. Cf. *Les Hierophantes*, by Fabre des Essarts. Chamuel, pub.
47. Read the very interesting work by Jules Bois: *Les Petites Églises.*
48. Extract from the Review *Paix Universelle* so valiantly directed at Lyon by our brother A. Bouvier.

Related Titles

from

Triad Press

The Pleromic Light Unveiled
By Tau Phosphoros

This short treatise examines the history, practice, and doctrine of the principal liturgy of the Apostolic Church of the Pleroma. Herein, Tau Phosphoros briefly explores each portion of the Mass, from the Preliminary Rites to the Dismissal, offering important practical notes and useful insights into its history, application, and the esoteric principles underlying each section. This work will be of great benefit to both the members of clergy who are celebrating or assisting in the Mass, and the congregants participating in its benediction.

Apostolic Church of the Pleroma Clergy Handbook
By Tau Phosphoros

The ACP Clergy Handbook is an invaluable tool for Gnostic clergy in formation. It is a useful reference book for all levels of clergy, and a fascinating glimpse into Gnostic theology, exegesis, history, and liturgical practice for anyone interested in ecclesiastical Gnosticism. Included are liturgies, theurgic operations, theoretical studies, and a comprehensive outline of the entire Minor Orders curriculum. Also includes the full text of The Kybalion and the Sepher Yetzirah.

Apostolic Church of the Pleroma Lectionary for Mass
By Tau Phosphoros

The ACP Lectionary contains three complete years of full-text liturgical readings for Sundays and other select Feast Days. This lectionary is intended for use with The Holy Gnostic Liturgy of the Pleromic Light (included) but may be easily adapted for use within other Gnostic liturgies.

Abbé Julio: His Life, His Work, His Doctrine
By Robert Ambelain, Translated and introduced by Tau Phosphoros

This concise work by the late bishop Robert Ambelain gives the details of the remarkable life and work of Abbé Julio, from hero of the Franco-Prussian War, to ostracized priest of the Roman Catholic Church, to priest-healer extraordinaire and archbishop metropolitan of the Eglise Catholique Française. In addition to the historical brief, Ambelain also gives a thoughtful exposition of the doctrine of Abbé Julio, arguing convincingly for a neo-Origenian theology. Also included are 15 of Abbé Julio's most powerful prayers, making this work not only informative, but practical. This is a great primer for anyone not familiar with Abbé Julio's life and works, and a valuable addition to the library of every current follower of the preeminent priest-healer.

Grand Marvelous Secrets
By Abbé, Translated and introduced by Tau Phosphoros

This work is the first volume of the 3-part opus of Abbé Julio. Contained within are prayers, blessings, Psalms, and exorcisms for all types of conditions, diseases, demonic oppression, and possession, and for every physical, mental, and spiritual well-being. The operations for every case are meticulously indexed in the back of this rare tome, available in its entirety in English for the first time.

The Little Religions of Paris
By Jules Bois, Translated by Tau Phosphoros

In The Little Religions of Paris French author, journalist, and playwright Jules Bois briefly examines some of the lesser-known religious sects percolating in the environs of fin-de-siècle Paris. Originally published in 1894, this work surveys such movements as the Theosophists, the Buddhists, the Swedenborgians, and of course the Gnostics. Even included herein are the Humanist cult of sociology pioneer Auguste Comte, and the later-discredited Palladian conspiracy of Leo Taxil, as well as several other interesting groups. This small volume provides an important snapshot of religious thought in the belle époch.

Exegesis of the Soul

Three Treatises on the
Nature, Origin, & Destiny
of the Human Soul

PAPUS

Exegesis of the Soul: Three Treatises on the Nature,
Origin, & Destiny of the Human Soul
By Papus, Translated and introduced by Tau Phosphoros

This special compilation collects three previously untranslated works by Papus:
- The Human Soul Before Birth and After Death (1898) is a fascinating exegesis on the Amélineau translation of the Pistis Sophia.
- How Is the Human Being Constituted? (1900) offers a thorough summary of the constituent parts of the human being: body, soul, and spirit, examining the unique function of each and how they work together to form a cohesive whole.
- What Becomes of Our Dead (1914), written in the midst of the horrors of the First World War, makes a contemplative analysis of the faculties and evolution of the human soul.
This volume is a must-have for every Gnostic and Martinist.

What is Occultism? It's Secrets and Reasons
By Papus, Translated and introduced by Sar Phosphoros

Papus, in his customary succinct yet erudite style, introduces the reader to the major tenets of traditional occultism. A remarkable amount of information is packed into this little work. With chapter headings such as: Theory, Metaphysics, Logic, Moral, Aesthetics, Theodicy, Sociology, etc., etc., this work touches upon all of the fundamentals of occult thought, including traditional history, practical occultism, and social reform. The beginner will find this to be a particularly useful guide while navigating his or her studies. There is much to be found here that is normally only introduced within the traditional initiatic fraternities and societies.

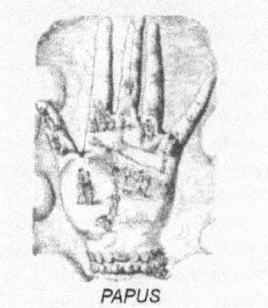

HOW TO READ HANDS
First Elements of Chiromancy

PAPUS

How to Read Hands: First Elements of Chiromancy
By Papus, Translated by Sar Phosphoros

Papus gives here a clear and concise introduction to the art and science of chiromancy, or palm reading. This work is highly informative, well-illustrated, and easy to follow. This is a great primer for beginners wishing to take up a serious study, or for those merely curious as to the fundamental principles. Several classic works on the subject are referenced here for further study.

What a Master Mason Ought to Know
By Papus, Translated by Sar Phosphoros

In this 1910 work, Papus collects some of his previous writings concerning the multiple facets of French Masonry and offers some new and insightful thoughts as well. He draws in part from the knowledge he received from such Masonic luminaries as John Yarker and W. W. Wescott. This work contains historical essays, mystical exegeses, Blue Lodge degree lectures, and much else of interest to the mystical Mason and Martinist.

Martinès de Pasqually: His life, His magical practices, His work, His disciples
By Papus, Translated by Sar Phosphoros

This seminal work by Papus looks at the life and teachings of the founder of the Elus Coens through examinations of the personal correspondence of the master with his disciples, whom he calls "emulators." This volume makes an excellent companion to the work of Le Forestier, containing much of the source material upon which the latter relies. Papus includes as an appendix some of the catechisms of the Elus Coens, which further elucidate Pasqually's doctrine of reintegration.

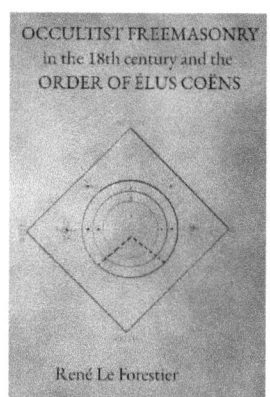

Occultist Freemasonry in the 18th Century
and the Order of Élus Coëns
by René Le Forestier, Translated by Sar Phosphoros

This classic tome is considered by many to be the definitive analysis of one of the most mysterious and enigmatic, yet one of the most influential orders of esoteric Freemasonry. Le Forestier carefully examines the doctrine, rituals, and history of this theurgical order par excellence of the 18th century. This will be of particular interest not only to every student of Martinism, but also to the students of the early development of the so-called Scottish degrees in France.

Masonic Orthodoxy: Followed by Occult
Masonry and Hermetic Initiation
By Jean-Marie Ragon, Translated and Introduced by Sar Phosphoros

This classic tome on Masonic history and doctrine is available in English for the first time since its publication in 1853. This important work is often referenced by Masonic historians. Indeed, most English-speaking Masonic enthusiasts are familiar with the name of Ragon, but very few have read his principal work. Every student of Masonic and para-Masonic organizations will want this volume on their shelves.

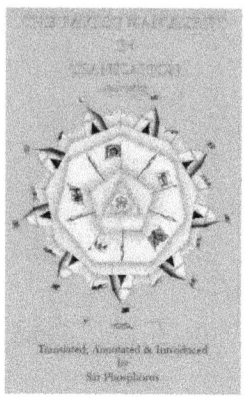

The Baylot Manuscript in Translation
Translated, Annotated, and Introduced by Sar Phosphoros

This rare manuscript of French Masonic rituals, drafted between the early 1750s and the late 1760s, containing a final date of 1768, is made available in English for the first time. This codex of over 30 unique pieces, spread across more than 70 folios, has been the subject of study and speculation among Masonic scholars for decades. Although the collection was assembled by and/or for the mysterious theurgist Martinès de Pasqually (founder of the influential Ordre des Chevaliers Maçons Elus Coëns l'Univers, the teachings and traditions of which would be carried on by his principal students Jean-Baptiste Willermoz, who would incorporate them into the upper ranks of his Rectified Scottish Masonry, and Louis-Claude de Saint-Martin, prolific author on mystical subjects under the nom de plume le Philosophe Inconnu), the present manuscript has little to do with his theurgic Masonry of Elect Priests, except for two catechisms near the end of the ms., and a tracing board of Coën design. It is, however, a compendium of early versions of Scottish or "écossais" grades that would become well known later as part of the Ancient & Accepted Scottish Rite. There are also some little-known grades, and some entirely unheard of in any other manuscript collections. Given the catalogue number of FM4 15 in France's Bibliotèque Nationale, this English-language translation of the French text will be a welcome addition to every serious student of the history of "High Grade" Freemasonry.

The Arcane Schools
By John Yarker Jr.

This hardbound edition of Yarker's classic opus is not merely another facsimile edition. It has been completely reformatted, yet retains a look and feel that is comparable to the original 1909 edition, right down to the blue cloth binding and gold stamped spine. From Alchemy to Zoroaster, and everything in between, The Arcane Schools continues to be one of the most comprehensive and authoritative works concerning the history and migration of the Western Mystery Tradition. Students of Freemasonry, Rosicrucianism, and Theosophy will find this to be an indispensable addition to their collection.

Brother of the Third Degree
By Will L Garver

Triad Press is proud to offer this hardcover clothbound edition of Brother of the Third Degree as part of our "Classics of the Western Mystery Tradition" series. Originally published in 1894, this volume continues to inspire seekers on the initiatic path as well as those who are fascinated with the Western Mysteries. While this volume contains a fictionalized account of initiation, those with eyes to see and ears to hear will recognize that a wealth of hermetic and esoteric principles are revealed within its prose.

The Holy Fire of St. Michael
By Richard Michael Willoughby

Gnostic poet and cleric Richard Michael Willoughby transcends the rational and offers a rare glimpse of modern Gnostic revelation, poetically exploring the heights and depths of spiritual awareness.

The Historical Pivot: Philosophy of History
In Hegel, Schelling, and Hölderlin
By William Andrew Behun

This work undertakes to demonstrate an emergent form of philosophy of history in German Idealism and Early German Romanticism, particularly focusing on the works of Hegel, Schelling, and Hölderlin. For these thinkers, history comes into its own as a topic of philosophical investigating. Breaking with the static historicism of the Enlightenment, German Idealist and Early German Romantic thinkers posit the idea of a constantly developing and emerging history and of the historical character of reality itself. The philosophy of history that comes out of the tradition of German Idealism as expressed by Schelling, Hegel and Hölderlin is deeply rooted in mythology, particularly the idea of a "Golden Age," which is both past and future.

www.ingramcontent.com/pod-product-compliance
Lightning Source LLC
Chambersburg PA
CBHW020958090426
42736CB00010B/1377